The Gnome Project

THE GNOME PROJECT

One Woman's Wild and Woolly Adventure

Jessica Peill-Meininghaus

Published by The Countryman Press, P.O. Box 748,
Woodstock, VT 05091
a division of W. W. Norton & Company, Inc.,
500 Fifth Avenue, New York, NY 10110
Printed in China through Asia Pacific Offset

The Gnome Project
978-1-58157-286-5

10 9 8 7 6 5 4 3 2 1

To anyone who has ever thought
that they couldn't . . .

Contents

A Note from the Author

*Y**ou're probably wondering* what sort of a madwoman would write a book about making gnomes for an entire year. Who is this woman? And why on earth would she make *gnomes*, of all things?

Let's deal with the madness piece first. The rest will come together on its own.

Many years ago, I decided to enter a wool painting into a contest at a fiber festival. Over the phone I gushed and tripped over myself in my enthusiasm, trying to tell the woman on the other end about the path that had led to this phone call. She waited patiently for me to finish and then asked what method I'd used to create the piece. When I replied, "I'm a needle felter," she sighed and responded, "Of course you are. All the needle felters I've met are a little bit crazy."

I have no idea about other needle felters — I tend to refer to them as "fabulous" — but "a little bit crazy" pretty much sums me up.

I'm certainly a little bit crazy about felting and gnomes—and a variety of other things in this world — but felting and gnomes took a unique turn in the scheme of things, and that's part of what this book is about.

I love hearing other people's stories. The questions *Where did we come from? How did we get here?* and *What about all the messy bits in between?* are some of my favorites to explore. So when I sat down to write this book, I did it with my children in mind. I wanted to answer those questions for them, give them an example of how we can change, and show them the road one person they knew very well traveled to get there. I wanted to remind them that we are more powerful than we give ourselves credit for.

This book is really about those messy bits most of all. I was pretty fed up with saying I'd do something and then not doing it — like becoming vegetarian only to be brought down by an insane fondness for breakfast sausage. I cannot tell you how much I *needed* to change.

So I decided that I needed a daily practice and that it would be making gnomes. And I made them, almost every day, for a year and beyond. Gnomes that I wasn't very excited about making, even though I loved them. Gnomes that made me cranky and frustrated and annoyed — before they transformed not only the way I saw my days, but also the way I saw myself and my life. I blogged about these gnomes. I named them and gave them unique personalities and life stories. I made them as real as I could manage, even though they only seemed to make me a little bit more crazy than I had been before.

I learned that the beginning of a daily practice is like climbing a mountain or going for a hike for the first time. There are aches and pains and frustrations and you pull things (namely muscles — both literal and figurative), and sometimes you might scream or swear like a sailor. And you can't tell how far you have to go because you can't see the top, and you *really* want to turn around and go back home. But in the end, if you keep pushing, you eventually get past all that (or most of it) — and that's when you start to see that it really *is* about the journey. The rhythm and peace that a daily practice brings are quite astonishing, and I don't think I could ever go back to a life without one.

I've always felt that creating art is, in and of itself, transformative, but I have discovered that when you endeavor to make art every day, you add to the power of that transformation. What this means is that no matter what happened in that day — whether you had a headache or received a bouquet of flowers — you sat

down and practiced one thing in the midst of that space in your life. One thing held true like a golden thread weaving your days together, giving you a bit of predictability through the chaos of the human experience.

The word *practice* used to make me cringe. I didn't feel that I had the time for it; I wanted everything to be perfect, *now*. But *practice* has become a gentle word to me. It doesn't have prerequisites, it doesn't demand a specific level of expertise or expectation; like the best teachers, practice simply encourages us to keep trying and doing our best. "Practice makes perfect" is transformed into "Practice *is* perfect." Who knew?

This is the story about how felting gnomes changed everything.

Well, maybe not *everything*. I'm still a little bit crazy.

The Museum of Unfinished Works

As far back as I can remember, I have never finished anything — not a darn thing — not unless someone made sure that I did with the fierceness of a schoolmarm or the enticement of sweets at the end.

For years, my mother's attic was a veritable museum of my unfinished works: a rug-hooking project gone wrong from when I was ten; the map of the United States that I started embroidering when I was twelve; and drawings, poems, and sewing and crafting projects from various ages. The list was long and, quite frankly, embarrassing, and it was all tucked away in labeled boxes with the good intention to finish someday. Everyone knows how it goes with good intentions, so let's not go there, shall we? Mine just didn't go. At all.

Eventually, my mother and I purged most of it, tossing it out or, if it was usable, donating it to a thrift store.

All except that half-embroidered map. *That* is still in a drawer somewhere in my house waiting to be completed, a ghost of what it surely could become.

I kept thinking I would grow out of this strange incapacity to finish anything, the way you grow out of a pair of pants or sucking your thumb. Eventually, I would know what I needed to do to follow through. It would come to me like an epiphany, and I would suddenly be one of "those people." You know the type — the kind of person who is fully capable of saying she is going to do something and then actually doing it. A real grown-up.

I'd seen others manage this feat, whether it was the lofty goal of learning a second language with the fluidity of a native or reading a new book every single month (or week . . . or day), or something as simple as going for a daily walk.

All around me there were people making goals for themselves and accomplishing them. Sometimes they did it without a backward glance. Sometimes they hit a few faltering steps before finding their stride — but they *always* seemed to find their stride. And then there were those who executed follow-through with so much grace that I wanted to scream at them and tell them to stop making something so tragically difficult look so darn easy.

When a high school friend started running daily, I felt the inspiration to get into shape and join in this new endeavor, albeit solo since we lived in different neighborhoods. I tied on some sneakers and took to the pavement. I lasted two days. The pain combined with the mere thought of forcing myself to endure another moment of discomfort was too much. Sure, I would eventually be fit enough that running would feel amazing, but I wasn't going to make it that far.

Then there was the time I decided to study marine biology. I went to the library, loaded up on the books they had, ordered the books they didn't, and went home to begin. Begin is all I did. That endeavor lasted about a week. I fell into the pattern of *I'll do that later, right now I want to be outside/watch a movie/hang out with a friend*. You get the picture.

My particular brand of disability didn't seem to affect everything. It didn't affect my schoolwork. In an effort to please my teachers and have a stellar transcript, I completed every single extra credit assignment they offered. Meeting deadlines for reports and finishing work issued by my teachers was pretty much a walk in the park. But the stuff that my friends managed on their own: exercising or keeping a daily journal or learning to play the guitar, using only their steadfast initiative to keep them engaged? That eluded me.

If I was accountable to someone, I could get the job done. But as soon as the commands were being issued only by me? Well, that was an entirely different story. If it didn't profit my family or friends in some way or another — and by *profit* I mean joy or money or food — I couldn't do it.

As a single person, you learn to adjust. You go to work, you read a book, you make dinner — you avoid situations that might bring on that feeling of failure. For me, that meant that I tried not to set goals, but even that wasn't something I could stick to. As humans, we are constantly striving to learn and change and evolve — you might even go so far as to say that we can't help but be capricious. I'm not any different. Still, despite a history of unmet goals, I strove to accomplish project after project on my own, and I failed over and over again.

When I got married and children came along, I managed well enough. Pregnancy was easy, if you overlook the hyperemesis. Along with the extreme nausea and vomiting, my body did what it wanted, regardless of my personal preferences on the matter, and babies were just that: babies. I wore them in slings, nursed them when they were hungry, and tried to steal sleep when they slept. There wasn't a need for follow-through; there were just instinctual answers to primal needs that create the unique bond between parent and infant. I could do that in my sleep — and about half the time, I did.

It was when the children grew older, when they could walk and talk and yell "Mine!" or "No!" and begin to struggle with the way the world works, that I discovered how incredibly important follow-through is. In fact, it is indispensable. When my children hit that stage, suddenly my lack of follow-through affected more than just me. It became a disability, like having one arm. I couldn't keep things in check.

It was time to seek the help of an expert.

Martha Stewart Meets the Goodwill Goddess

delia knows follow-through. In fact, she knows it so well, it is as if she has merged with it, providing a physical body in which follow-through can hang out and make the rest of the world jealous. Whenever I stopped by, her house was, without fail, spotless and organized. It was Martha Stewart meets the Goodwill Goddess, and like Mary Poppins, it was practically perfect in every way.

The couch, used but carefully covered with a lovely blanket, was smooth without a wrinkle in sight, and plump pillows had been issued to each end, set neatly, at an angle, into the corners. The rugs were vacuumed, and the curtains were even and opened appropriately for the amount of light at that particular moment in the day. The kitchen was organized and clean, and the floors were freshly mopped. The houseplants thrived, flashing their lush, radiant foliage from their various, carefully chosen perches. And Adelia had a child. Granted, there was only the one to my four, but she did have a child, so the well-worn argument of "Well, it looks like that now, but wait until she has kids" wouldn't fly.

I was constantly struck by Adelia's ability to keep things in check. Inspired, I would go home and re-organize every room until the house glowed with perfection. I trimmed and watered the houseplants that were limping along. I vacuumed, mopped, and made beds. Everything would look perfect . . . for about two days, and sometimes as long as a week. But eventually, my inability to follow through would kick in and things would unravel.

Suddenly, there were ailing, thirsty plants. Laundry piled up so high that, much like Mount Everest, it was a task definitely not to be attempted without train-ing. Then there were the papers, toys, and goodness knows what else covering every surface. My husband, Jens, creative man that he is, dubbed this condition Empty Surface Syndrome. ESS meant that as soon as a surface was cleared and empty, something else would immediately appear, drawn to the pristine location as if there were a strange magnetic force at work.

Time and again, my inherent lack of

follow-through set me up for failure. Sure, I could get the house clean and organized, but I couldn't seem to *keep* it clean and organized.

Disheartened, I finally went to Adelia and asked her point-blank how she did it. She smiled a kind but perhaps (unless my jealous mind imagined it) superior smile and sat down on her wrinkle-free couch.

"I just decide what days I will do which tasks. I choose one day for each big task and a part of each day for the daily tasks so everything gets done. I make my bed every morning and clean my room. I never go to bed without the dishes done and the kitchen completely clean. I smooth the couch blanket every time I walk by. I vacuum and sweep in the afternoon. I wash the bathroom once a week on Saturdays. I just maintain everything. Oh, and I water my plants every Wednesday. I call it Water Wednesdays."

I nodded and looked around at her perfect home. Suddenly everything seemed so manageable and easy as her words sank in.

"Okay. That makes sense. A day for everything, a time for everything. I can do that."

I went home and reorganized the house, purged anything extra that had wheedled its way into our home, and looked around at the perfectly clean environment I was so committed to maintaining. And I tried again.

I watered on Wednesday. I vacuumed every afternoon. I washed the bathroom on Saturday. I made my bed, and those of the children, every morning. I fluffed my couch cushions and I washed the dishes. I cleaned the kitchen every night; I even mopped. I did all of this with great diligence. For about one week. And then, as my life of nursing multiple children and cooking meals and milking goats and collecting eggs from over fifty chickens went on in the way life does, my good intentions were knocked down one by one.

First, it was the fluffing of the cushions. *Just this once I'll skip it and sit. I'm so tired!* And then it was the mopping. *I'll do that tomorrow.* And then the dishes: *I just made a batch of cheese and baked bread and the baby's napping. I should lie down while I have a chance.* Then the bed, the last casualty of my good intentions: *Why make the bed when I am going to get back into it later today? Just for today I'll skip it.*

It was the slippery slope, the moment before I plummeted off the edge of the precarious, well-organized cliff into the familiar of the undone existence. I would make household rules about discipline and establish consequences: "If you don't do your chores during the week, you can't watch the Friday night movie." Or, "Don't eat on the furniture or you won't be welcome to sit on it." But I would either promptly forget or feel too overwhelmed to enforce any of them.

No amount of resolution, the New Year's variety or any other, seemed to do a thing. Soon I began to fully believe that I was incapable — that somehow I had been born without the gene for completion and self-discipline, and I would have to limp along through life, leaving a trail of unfinished chores in my wake.

After a lifetime of this frustration, I developed several other complicating factors, including an underlying lack of trust in my ability to achieve *anything*. Full stop. And the belief that I wasn't a grown-up at all. What mature human would leave so many things undone? What sort of effective parent could I possibly be? My children were doomed because of what I lacked.

As I puzzled over my situation, it occurred to me that I had set myself up for failure yet again. Keep the entire house as clean and organized as Adelia's pristine home? What was I thinking?

I needed to start with something small. Very, very *small*.

The
Daily Practice

*M**any people in this world have a daily* practice. They exercise, they drink the same tea, they stretch, they do yoga, they meditate, they walk the dog, they practice an instrument — the list is long and varied. Meanwhile, I eat, sleep, drink, go to the bathroom, attempt to meet my children's ever-changing needs, make art, and wish like a fiend for something more.

There are still great things I feel I must do in this life. There are the endangered elephants and whales I wish to save, and I can't forget the plight of the orangutans. There are the people around the world in great need, if only I could find a way to help them. There are people everywhere living in art-deficient communities that could use a boost. And oceans that need cleaning and a planet that needs championing. But with four kids to raise, those things would have to wait, and a daily practice seemed like something that would be good. If I couldn't be out there with Greenpeace, throwing myself in front of whaling ships, perhaps I could learn a second language — or take a walk. I had to remind myself to think small.

I admired the staunch determination that it took to make something happen every single day. I had a teacher tell me once that her father believed in rhythm and habit so strongly that he ate a peanut butter and jelly sandwich for lunch every day for thirty years. Thirty years? After two days, I'd be climbing the walls and throwing together a grilled cheese sandwich or some curry. I needed things to be different, and yet I craved something in that daily PB&J world her father lived in.

I imagined that one would feel "held" by that rhythm, finding contentment and safety in knowing what was to come, perhaps an armor of protection in knowing the way the world worked, if only in the facet of what you were going to eat for lunch. I craved the peace of mind that I believed came when you had something predictable in your day that was a chosen element.

Thomas Jefferson wrote: "Whether I retire to bed early or late, I rise with the sun." His was a small daily practice but one that was consistent and rewarding for him for fifty years. Some people say that having one thing you do with consciousness and purpose, every single day, will bring rewards. Those rewards vary depending on what it is that you are doing, but there *will* be rewards. I could only imagine what they would be for me.

So, on January 8, I made what I thought was a small, innocent, and completely innocuous decision to make one gnome every day for a year. The next twelve months would have been very, very different if not for that decision.

A Thing
for Gnomes

s an artist, I make my art — more specific- ally, tapestries — out of wool roving, which is wool that has been cleaned, carded, usually dyed, and most often comes rolled into balls like yarn, only much thicker and not spun the way yarn is. Using a special barbed needle, aptly called a felting needle, I poke the wool with a jabbing motion, locking the fibers together and creating sculptures, pictures, and much more. The pesky barbs on the end of the needle do most of the work; I just have to remember to keep my fingers away from them or keep Band-Aids on hand. The versatility of subjects has a way of keeping me happy with this particular medium. Whether it's bun- nies in dresses or overalls, or dragons or deities or flappers, I can easily switch if things get too mundane.

I've always had a thing for gnomes. I can't quite pinpoint when the fascination began, but it's rooted somewhere deep in my childhood, back in a time when I believed that if I soared high enough on the swing in the backyard, I would find myself flying to Africa on the back of a unicorn with a gnome, a fairy, and my brother as companions. The idea that a gnome could, at any given moment, be doing good deeds, healing sick animals, or playing harmless pranks, all while hidden away from human sight, was appealing. Their twinkling eyes, pointy hats, (or toadstool caps), and bushy beards were just icing on the cake. I was hooked.

But I'm picky about what my gnomes look like. They have to fall into a category that you might refer to as "charming." When I first started felting gnomes, I wanted them to be up to my annoyingly high standards. They couldn't just have pointy hats and bushy white beards and be vaguely gnome-esque. They needed to have a certain presence — an expression and personality. They needed to be something that would make me smile. I also wanted them to be simple enough that I wouldn't spend hours trying to create a wool version of a tiny Botticelli face, delicately fingered hands, and grossly overdetailed boots on a figure only four inches tall. None of that was going to work if I wanted to sell them at an affordable price and still keep my sanity.

It took me a while to figure out how to do this. The first ones were kind of charming but too simple, sporting an indented line for the eyes but no other facial features and no nose.

Then slowly, over time, they evolved.

There were no directions or how-to guides for me to follow, so there was a distinct learning curve that resembled a ride on a roller coaster. At first, it was fun. Then it was sort of boring. And then, I hate to admit it, it was annoying. Those gnomes did something I wasn't too happy about: They challenged me. Like a child who can't sit still, I was antsy and restless in the face of their sameness. In the past, the only endeavors I stuck with were the ones that allowed for some shifting of sequence. They also had to be very small, short-term projects. If it was knitting a sweater for myself or a friend, forget about it. But if it was knitting a baby hat with several colors, I could work my way through. After all, children grow fast, so I had to finish it promptly or it wouldn't fit.

THE gnome PROJECT

I chose different colors, and no two gnomes could ever be *exactly* alike, but in the end gnome-making meant making a version of the same thing over and over again, and that wasn't going to fly.

Though I liked the outcome — all those little gnomes looking back at me — I didn't revel in the process of it. The gnomes made me sit and that was annoying. So I went back to making tapestries, where I could switch subjects and forms as often as I felt the urge, and I stopped making gnomes. I couldn't keep making something that I found so unfulfilling, right? Right.

The thing was, I had already taken my gnomes to a couple of craft fairs in some of our local schools, and they had sold out. It didn't occur to me that this would cause a problem, but it did. I would be vending at a fair, and someone would come up and say, "Oh! You're the gnome lady! Do you have any gnomes? I'd love to get a couple!" and I would smile weakly and say, "I'm so sorry, I don't have any right now."

No businesswoman ever got successful by ceasing production of her most popular product. I'm not a financial success story — I'm a frugal artist, careful, but not necessarily financially prosperous . That never mattered, since I wasn't in it for the money.

Fast-forward several months to when I found myself undergoing a minor surgical procedure to repair a femoral hernia and was laid up on Vicodin for a week. Now, I was raised on homeopathic medicine and herbal tea. I treated my children, my husband, and myself for the swine flu and myriad other illnesses with herbs and homeopathics, and they've served us well. I almost never take ibuprofen, though there are moments when it is completely indispensable. So Vicodin was a whole new beast. For those of you who have never tried it, it's an entirely different kind of drug. It isn't really a painkiller. It doesn't take the pain away. You just don't care that you are in pain. When you're on it, everything is beautiful and easy but in a distant, I-may-not-really-be-here sort of way that is very uncomfortable.

Vicodin did something else for me as well. Not only did I not care about the painful slice in the line of my hip joint, I also didn't care about the monotony of gnome-making. I could make gnomes all day and not bat an eye. It was very strange, even if I was only vaguely aware of the strangeness.

So I began making gnomes by the truckload. I watched Jane Austen movies and British sitcoms and made gnomes all day, every day — for a whole week.

Then I called my doctor and said, "You've got to take me off this stuff! I like it way too much, and I am far more productive than I have ever been with the things I like the least. *That's not a good sign.*

Can I go on ibuprofen now?" And just like that, I was off the juice.

Initially I was glad, but then I saw the bag of fifty gnome heads I had made while in my stupor, and I was annoyed. I couldn't just leave them there, *bodiless*. The holidays were coming and people would probably buy them, and now I had a surgery to pay for, so I had to finish them. I considered the Vicodin again, but I could not conceive of taking any more of a drug I did not medically need in order to produce small replicas of an elusive elemental often seen in the British Isles. Instead I hunkered down, gave the heads some bodies, and called it good.

Good
Intentions

*I*t was this loathing of making the same thing over and over that inspired my choice of gnome-making as a daily practice. I knew I had to choose something that I didn't really want to do but could do easily. It couldn't be something as simple as "Breathe" because obviously I would be a giant success story without having earned it. It couldn't be really hard like "Run a Marathon," though, or my failure would only add to my shame. It had to be something that found a happy medium between personal challenge and simplicity of execution, and I instinctively knew it couldn't be something that I "should" do, such as a daily workout or furthering my literary knowledge with a book a week. That would put too much pressure on me, and under pressure I might bolt straight out of my good intentions.

My mother once told me that the youngest of my four aunts chose to study in school the subject that was the hardest for her, the one that challenged her the most. I was very little when she told me this, but I have often thought of it and wondered whether I could ever be strong enough to choose something that pushes all my buttons and still follow through with it if no one was making me do it.

Gnomes weren't algebra or trigonometry, but they made me sit and repeat, two things that I did not like to do. They stilled me while I was in the process of creating. They also didn't take more than an hour, so I could, realistically, manage to make time in every day to create one. I'm a visual person, and I could also *see* the fruits of my labor, perhaps prompting more success. Of course, I might sell a few along the way, and that would be good for our bank account.

The longest daily practice I had ever experienced to this point was the conscious choice to stretch every morning. That lasted about three months. A record but, by my standards, absolutely pathetic. Working out was a joke that had never lasted, either. So when I sat there, eight days into the new year, and thought, *I'll make a gnome every day for a year*, what I was really thinking was, *I'll last about a month — if I'm lucky — but I might as well.* And then, well, then the magic of the technological age gave me a nudge and whispered, *You might last longer if you blog about it.*

And things started to shift, just fractions of an inch. But they did, indeed, shift.

It wouldn't hurt to try.

So I made one little gnome, took his photo, and posted him on the blog. It was interesting to see that single little gnome perched on a plant staring out at me from the computer screen.

I typed in the words "Here. We. GOOOOOOOO!" and signed off.

And then I waited for Day 2.

6

That "I Can!"
Attitude

y the time Day 3 arrived, I had loosened up enough to add a little something about who I thought this gnome might be, including suspected personality traits.

Day 3 gnome, at left, is flamboyant and jolly in those pink and blue crisscross leggings and that bright lime shirt. I am certain his core goal is the spreading of impish merriment.

I held little trust in my ability to achieve much more, so I made light of my gnome-making project and didn't tell anyone other than Jens for the first week or so. The fewer who witnessed my failure, the better. I didn't need a peanut gallery on this one.

My youngest child, who was eight, examined each one in turn, always proclaiming the newest to be better than its predecessors. And though there was some definite eye-rolling from the older children about their whack-job mom's attempt at an epic gnome-making project, for the most part they were curious and encouraging, taking moments to peek at my gnome stash and either shake their heads or smile. My fourteen-year-old, the oldest and the only boy, even wrote a poem for me titled "The Gnome Lady."

At the beginning of any project, there is that enthusiasm — the *I can!* attitude that gets the job done — and I had that driving force pulsing through my veins. But fifty-two weeks? *Twelve months of gnomes?* That was 365 — no, 2012 was a leap year, 366 — gnomes to make. That was surely crazy talk.

This wasn't an order for a customer. This wasn't to prepare for a fair. There wouldn't be any assembly line on this. This was about making one gnome from scratch, from tip of hat to toe, every day without cutting corners. That was at once intimidating, exhilarating, and — when it came to my artist's need for change — absolutely horrifying. And though the idea occurred to me that placing gnomes in trees and on doorsteps throughout the city would be quite a lark, this wasn't about gnomefying the world. This was about a daily practice, something I had to commit myself to, come hell or high water.

This was an adventure. It was new and exciting, though I quickly discovered that I had to schedule each gnome. It wasn't that I was so busy with endless lists of chores. It was that this one task was enough to throw me off for the entire day. It only took about a week for that gnome of the day to loom over me like impending incarceration, sucking the entire day into his four-inch body and swallowing my freedom whole.

I cursed them, even as I made them one by one, wondering how I could be held captive by something so small, so innocuous, and so easily put aside and ignored.

The gnomes were little and silly. They were what one dear friend referred to as a "gimme" — something small, inexpensive, and easily produced on a large scale. But I made them, putting as much change as I could manage into every one. They wore different colors, and each, as always, had a different face and beard and hat.

I held fast until Day 12, when I woke up and realized that I had not made a gnome the day before. That's when I discovered that while this project was sort of silly, not something that would save orangutans or

create world peace, it had done something that no other practice had managed thus far: It had begun to embed.

Perhaps it was because I didn't care, at least on the surface. Or perhaps it was because I wasn't hanging a lot of hope on the gnomes. But when I woke up on Day 12 and realized that I hadn't even blinked, hadn't noticed one iota that there hadn't been a gnome on Day 11, I actually teared up. I was angry that I had been so thoughtless in this place in myself where I wanted so dearly to have thought. And I melted. I indulged in some self-flagellation on the matter, reaming myself over and over.

DAY
9

It is through our mistakes that we grow and learn. I learned that I missed greatly that little part of the day. I missed it! What a wonderful thing to learn! In honor of Day 11's lack of gnome and as encouragement to myself, I decided a photograph of the gnomes that were made (and haven't sold!) would remind me about what the real goal of this whole experiment is and that, so far, I am doing just fine. I am off to embark on Day 12's gnome and re-establish the rhythm and peace that each little gnome brings into my day.

Jens, looking somewhat smug, said, "Honey, you can just make an extra one."

But I shook my head. "That isn't a daily practice. If I miss making a gnome for one day, then that day doesn't get a gnome. Period. I can't rewind. The day has passed, and it went without a gnome. I have to move on and do better."

I made myself a cup of tea, and then I made the gnome for Day 12. He was stabbed into existence with purpose.

Urban
Restlessness

anuary was a big month. It ushered in a year that promised more than the idea of the apocalypse and human spiritual evolution, and lots and lots of gnomes. It also brought a big change for my family. The change had stemmed from our quest for a simpler life and the intrinsic value this could hold for us. But to explain how this came to be, I have to back up and give a little more history about this wild journey.

In the early years of our marriage, Jens and I had moved from our tiny house in a growing city just north of Portland, Oregon, to a farm — or "farmlette" as we liked to call it, since it was only two acres — even farther north. On the farmlette was an old house, a barn, and animals. We had chickens (those would be the fifty mentioned earlier), goats, geese, ducks, a cow, and at one point a couple of pigs and a couple of sheep.

I was barefoot and pregnant (in the non-anti-feminist sort of way). I spent my days in the kitchen, making bread and concocting natural recipes and herbal remedies. I milked the goat in the morning and made cheese and hunted down eggs with the children in barn and field and bush. We homeschooled and made art and took long walks and didn't worry about money because we didn't spend any. We lived simply and frugally and became whole within that space in our lives.

Eventually we sold the farm and moved to Portland, a city that was lovely and exciting and had so much to offer that we were happy and content — for about six months. That's when the dreams started. The dreams where I went back to the farm weeping and asked the new owners to sell it back to us, showing them where my daughters had been born and waking with tears on my cheeks and such longing that I would cry all over again.

This went on for several years, and as those years passed, my husband and I grew increasingly restless in our urban setting. Finally we agreed that when the housing market recovered we would sell and move. Until then we would have to make do with farming in the city.

The apple trees went in, then the currants and elderberries, the blueberries and fig tree. The olive tree went in and then back out after the dog ate it. The grapes planted along the path and subsequent arbor thrived, forming a shaded path from the street. A greenhouse went up in the backyard, just a basic hoop house, but the first year we measured the tomatoes at nine feet tall. The shed turned into a yoga and meditation studio, and suddenly we had an oasis in the midst of the busyness and noise of the city.

But it wasn't enough. We couldn't see the stars at night — not clearly — not like they are in the country where the night is a black dome with tiny pinpricks of light. That's what we needed; that's what we dreamed of.

So, after seven years of dreaming and hoping, I took the plunge and called our mortgage company. Considering that we so often limped through the month, and the banks weren't so hip on loaning after the recession, I didn't think my endeavors would get us anywhere, but I needed to try. After about an hour, I got off the phone and stared at the notes I'd scribbled on the paper on the kitchen table. We were approved. I had no idea how or why, but we were, and I wasn't about to argue. We could buy a second home.

When you put it that way, it sounds super grand, doesn't it?

"Why, yes, we have this house as well as a *second* house. Just a moment, another one of my diamonds rolled under the couch, and I want to grab it before the maid comes in to vacuum. You know how it is."

Um, not quite. The second home could cost no more than a fancy new pickup truck. We're talking the housing prices of yesteryear. But we started looking anyway, determined to manifest exactly what we needed.

The West Coast was going to be tricky, considering the high cost of living and how popular it was. Even a broken-down, unlivable place was well out of our price range. Since my family lived in the East, we started looking there. We ran into ramshackle houses, grand places that had been gutted, hunting cabins, and a personal favorite: a place in Virginia on five acres with a cabin whose description simply read, "Property infested with snakes, buyers and realtors beware." (I'm totally serious, it really did.)

As I made this little gnome tonight, I kept thinking "Yellowpants Maggenty." I don't know why, but perhaps that is his name? Who knows. I just know that today wasn't complete until I had finished good ole Yellowpants.

DAY

16

There were far too many searches, emails, and phone calls for me to count. We hunted tirelessly through twelve states before we settled on Maine. It had many rural properties, was beautiful and rugged but refined, had easy access to the ocean, was close enough to family, and had properties so cheap I had to put my eyes back in their sockets more than once.

DAY
17

DAY
20

DAY
19

Eventually, I found a house that was so delicious and huge and beautiful that I was certain the price tag was missing a zero. I called my mother and said, "Forget mother-daughter dresses. Let's have mother-daughter houses. I'd only be about five hours away!" We gushed about it over the phone, and I sicced the real estate agent on it with ferocity. Surely there was something horribly wrong with it. It was on a floodplain or wasteland, or it needed a new foundation, or the septic tank or well was shot and needed replacing, or it was just a shell and needed everything. I waited on pins and needles for the agent, and when she called with the good news, my hands began to shake.

I could spend a whole chapter on the adventures that followed as we maneuvered the strange circumstances of getting the loan finalized and the house negotiated, but as exciting as it was to us then, it would be boring as hell to read now, so I'll just say that we jumped through many hoops and ended up with our dream home.

And through it all, I was making gnomes.

Keeping It
Interesting

As phone calls and emails were exchanged with a state three thousand miles away, gnomes accumulated in my box of inventory. Gnomes with striped pants and polka-dotted hats. Gnomes with white beards and brown beards. Girl gnomes and boy gnomes, young gnomes and old gnomes — and even small baby gnomes, which are all wool (no pipe cleaner) and which I dubbed "gnomelettes" and "gnomelings."

DAY
21

At the beginning of the year, I could have skipped making a gnome on my birthday. The little voice in my head said, *No one would blame you. It is your birthday.* But I didn't.

I made my birthday gnome and the gnomes on the other days, too, one by one as I made lists of what we needed from the house — manageable repairs, a working boiler, a clean title. And then I made lists of all we needed for the house, such as a generator, insulation, lumber, and siding. I slept on the lists, wedged under my pillow, in an effort to bring them into fruition and keep them at the forefront of my mind and heart and dreams.

It has been a challenging week. I sat down, very tired, to make a gnome, and suddenly the idea of bending the pipe cleaner seemed hard, not in the difficult meaning but the tactile one, and I craved a soft activity. I stumbled for a minute and then realized that a baby gnome is soft, no wire, no bending — they are all wool. They are tiny, and we all started off tiny and soft. I made this little baby gnome with a tuft of red hair and a pointed cap. A little bit of softness to remind the world of the roots we all share.

In February, when the waiting was almost too much to handle and the anticipation had me on the brink of developing a twitch, I challenged myself to make tiny gnomes, trying to see how small I could get them and still have them look like gnomes. It was all I could do to keep going with the project. One night, I was up so late — past midnight — that I made the gnome for one day, and then the next, and dubbed them "the Midnight Twins."

DAY
26

DAY
27

DAY 28

DAY 30

DAY 31

DAY 32

Desperate, in those first three months, to keep them exciting so that I wouldn't stop making them, I began to let the wool inspire me. I made a gnome with a mushroom toadstool cap and more baby gnomes.

DAY
37

DAY
41

DAY
40

I made gnomes with gray beards and gnomes with brown skin. In previous years, when I made dolls or gnomes, the ones with brown skin didn't sell as quickly, which I found very sad. The color of someone's skin shouldn't ever carry the weight that so many people put on it. Though so many gnomes I have made are fair-skinned, I often dream of dark-skinned gnomes — with close-cropped beards or long dreadlocks or cornrows. This would be hard to do with the size gnome I usually create, but one can always dream.

DAY

42

DAY

44

As the closing date on the house in Maine drew nearer, changed, and then was finalized, I put my hopes and my wishes, my frustrations and my tears into the gnomes of January and February. Through the long months of the gloomy Pacific Northwest winter, I tried to bring cheer into our cottage with my creations. This gnome is feisty and jolly like so many — but he is certainly himself in all that, a unique individual. He is a star catcher, this one...

DAY
45

DAY
48

DAY
50

DAY
52

DAY
53

They broke up what were sometimes depressing days of long phone calls and strong emotions. The children would sit next to me as I felted, and watch or read a book, then smile when I finished. Jens would settle onto the couch at the end of the day and listen with contentment for another day of practice accomplished, and mild annoyance at the perpetual *chk chk chk* sound of my needle. Friends would inquire about the gnomes when they stopped in for tea or to visit. Or they would ask if they could watch me make one while we laughed and chatted. A daily mantra of sorts developed, and I heard it chanted by the voices of those I loved in my head, asking: *Did you make a gnome today?* And even when I felt that I was far too exhausted by the speed at which life traveled around me, it was deeply satisfying to be able to answer with a resounding "Yes, I did."

Taking
Root

In March, when the cherry trees gracing our lovely city adorned themselves with flowers, and parting clouds teased us with a burst of warm weather and uncharacteristic sunshine, my mother came to visit.

DAY
60

DAY
62

DAY
63

DAY
64

Her arrival coincided beautifully with the signing of the final paperwork on the new house — and I made a gnome. All that work and stress and hope had culminated in the realization of a dream, and everything went into the gnome. He wore purple in various shades with swirls of lavender on his hat. I had heard once, long ago, that blue was the color of prosperity and red the color of love, so I figured purple would encompass both, but I never checked to see if that was true.

At the end of those first couple of months, I looked at my progress — so many gnomes lined up ready for new homes. I casually pointed it out to Jens, my mother, and a few close friends in that sort of desperate way that says, *See! See! I can follow through. Credit please!* But inside I was waiting for the other shoe to drop, for the panic or laziness or distraction to reach the point that I would skip it "just for today."

DAY
69

DAY
70

DAY
71

DAY
72

Not only was it a new moon, but it was a day of new and wonderful things, and when I sat down with the fire and Downton Abbey, *along came this fellow all mellow and purple and steeped in magic. I found myself doing curling, whirling symbols all over his purple cap and felt as though he had some new moon magic about him.*

As time went by and more people heard about the project, they would ask, "So, do you just make a bunch of heads and hats? That would be easier, to streamline it." And I would shake my head. "Nope, they have to be made from scratch. It's about the act of making one, not about the time involved."

It was in the making, the forming, the felting, and then the looking into the little face and seeing who lurked there. That is what it had become. I was surprised that I was still going. It was as if I had stepped outside of myself and was looking at someone else, someone who understood commitment. But it wasn't me. Surely it couldn't be.

THE *gnome* PROJECT

66

DAY
86

DAY
87

TAKING ROOT

67

Then, in early April, I missed Day 89.

I was really sick, and despite being desperately ill with a virus, I reamed myself for missing it before stopping, mid-lash, to take stock of what I had achieved instead of what I hadn't. Eighty-eight days of gnomes. Yes, I had missed two of them, but I had endeavored for that long. If I quit, I still would have that many days of a practice. It took some of the bitter taste of failure out of my mouth, and I rested and made sure there was a gnome for Day 90 (pictured at right).

He is a mellow fellow, prone to breaking out in poetry and occasional lyrical song. He loves ponds and enjoys the rising of the sun every day and the setting of the sun every evening.

DAY 91

DAY 92

DAY 93

DAY 94

*There was a late night arrival for a gnome
last night. She is tiny — a baby gnome —
a gnomeling. I couldn't help it, with the
aspect of walnut cradles, I was inspired to
make a teeny tiny gnomeling. I only have
the one cradle at the moment, but there
will be more. She is a scant ½ inch and she
is smiling — how can she not, being born in
the spring, as a gnome, among flowers??
She will do great things, this one.*

The gnomes were getting under my skin. They were fueling something inside me that I dared not look at. I was afraid that if I spent any time congratulating myself or took a moment to bask, I might stop. Sometimes I was up until almost midnight trying to fit my gnome in.

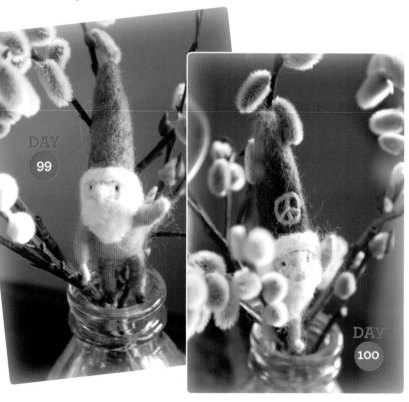

There were times when I focused on the colors of the season and tried to make the gnomes match the weather and feel of the day. On other days, I branched out and went for something out of the ordinary, such as a ninja gnome. And then there were days when I just made one to get it done.

DAY
104

DAY
105

I missed Days 106 and 107 to severe food poisoning. I thought of making the gnome on Day 106; I could see him in my head, but I could not find the physical ability to sit up and make him, so I slept. I slept right through making him and did the same the following day as well. I lay in bed shaking and trying not to vomit for two days until the salmon that had caused all that damage was out of my system, and I cried about those gnomes.

I was so disappointed and terrified — yes, I was actually terrified — that this was the beginning of a slippery slope that would end in another story about how I'd started a project but one thing led to another and it never got completed.

Meanwhile, my family seemed unfazed. For all intents and purposes, the gnome-making was just something that I did. They had no fear that it would end. It was as if I had always done this strange practice. But even with their confidence backing me up, I was full of doubt.

10

Tell Me
Something Good

It was also in April that my husband flew across the country to the new, never-before-seen-by-us house and called with updates as he fulfilled the requirements our insurance company had laid out for us.

"It's big. Really big, honey," he said when he called. "And it's trashed. It isn't livable right now. We have years of work ahead of us."

My heart pounded in response. "Crap! We put everything we had into it. Tell me something good. You're scaring me."

"Oh! Sorry, I just want to make sure you understand. Everything is just trashed and will need to be redone. But, honey, it's *beautiful*. It's the most amazing house. I've been here one day and I love it more than any house I've ever been in. It will be spectacular when it's done, but it may take twenty years."

DAY
108

DAY
109

DAY
111

DAY
110

I calmed my breathing and said, "Good. At least we won't get bored. Send me pictures."

"I will. Are you making a gnome? "

"How'd you know?" I asked.

"I can hear the *chk chk chk* of the needle," he said, and I could hear the smile in his voice over the phone.

DAY
113

DAY
114

After all those missed days, I was newly determined not to miss any more, so I kicked it up a notch in an effort to stay inspired and focused. I ventured into unknown territory when I made a *mer-gnome* — a creation I cooked up that was a mystical combination of mermaid and gnome, complete with hat and seaweed in his beard — that would certainly never sell.

It sold — within hours. So I made more of these strange mer-gnomes and built an inventory for the upcoming fairs.

At one school fair, a woman bought a gnome to take on a cruise. On the online Etsy shop, a mother bought one to photograph and write a story about for her young son. Children bought them for their parents and parents for their children, and I kept making them.

It has been a while since a gnomeling came about, and so I set to work. This one is a small helper of blossoms — that is to say that when this particular gnomeling is around, the blossoms are bigger, sweeter and last longer — it's this gnomeling's special power...

In between making gnomes and a few tapestries, I also packed and labeled boxes, and touched up paint here and there, all the while wondering how our house saga would play out. I ate, dreamed, and breathed ideas about the new old house so far away, waiting to be loved again.

After a day of playing and packing and, more often than I would like to admit, stressing, I would make a gnome. With a long history of going to bed at the same time as Jens and the kids, I began staying up alone, felting, and putting all my wonder and angst and confusion into every poke.

DAY
122

DAY
125

DAY
126

DAY
127

DAY
128

It was around this time that I tentatively began going to a water aerobics class at my local community center. Knowing my history, I didn't place much importance on it. After all, I probably wouldn't last more than two weeks. But it would be good for me while I did it, so I started going, one day at a time.

At first it was hard to drag myself up and out at five thirty in the morning, but soon I began to enjoy it. Water aerobics was hard work but surprisingly rewarding.

Each day I thought, *Only today. I'll probably quit in a week, but I'll try to go today.* I never put much pressure on myself — and soon I was going three times a week like clockwork. Imagine my surprise when I woke up, without alarm or prompting, and walked out the door for class week after week after week.

DAY
129

DAY
131

DAY 134

DAY 136

There were other changes, too. I began to establish a rule here and there about what could and could not happen in our home, and I followed through on it. When I said there could be no shoes worn in the house, suddenly I found socked feet pattering around the cottage floors. The stairs, so often riddled with piles of laundry and toys, were clear because, lo and behold, *that was the rule.* I began to find that, once I had stated the rule, following through was easier. I could recognize when something was not done, and if need be send a wayward, booted child back to the mudroom to tuck his or her galoshes under the bench. Or, I could find it in myself to remind one of my daughters that her books and a teddy bear were on the stairs where they did not belong.

All these years when other mothers in my life had found household rules easy to follow and uphold, I had struggled, tripping down clothing-sprinkled stairs, mopping floors muddied for the umpteenth time that day, and letting the coats pile on the bench in the entry-way. Now, as I looked around me at a house that held a semblance of order I had miraculously managed to create, I clung to the mantra that seemed to be working for me: *This is fleeting. It could all disintegrate in a matter of moments. But for right now, this is the way it is.*

A Gnome in
Lieu of Food

*T*hings were changing both outside and inside, and I was trying to stay present in my rhythm. The weather began to shift into that it-may-not-rain-forever stage that hits the Northwest, and we made some big decisions about our move.

With the housing market upside down, we realized that we couldn't sell and would instead need to rent out our little urban farm. This was no small task. New lists were made, and I spent days emailing and screening and interviewing prospective tenants, trying to find the people who would want to take on and truly care for the magical oasis that was our home. We finally signed the papers and began making plans for our cross-country road trip.

The first task was deciding what to keep and what to give away. My mother had generously assisted us in acquiring a moving van — of the you-load-it-we-drive-it

variety — and it felt like a novelty. But knowing that space was limited, as was the time to load and unload, the pressure built about what could go and what had to stay.

When I called a friend to come and take my carefully stored and coveted organic red quinoa and many other gluten-free goodies, I almost cried. We'd discovered that they wouldn't fit, and I figured I could easily replace it all once we had moved. (How wrong I was.)

We gave away the furniture and chairs and found storage for the few things too big to fit and too loved to give away: the roots grown around rocks we found in a river while camping one summer; the kitchen table made from salvaged fir flooring a hundred years old, polished to rosy-red glory; and so much more. And, in the midst of the chaos, I still made gnomes. On too many days, it was the thing I looked forward to the most, something that held me together. Part of my life was being thrust into the Unknown while another part was building momentum for that new adventure, and though this was all a path I was choosing, it made me both mournful and joyful, in turn. That daily gnome gave me time to just be where I was — whether it was fighting the fear or cuddling up to it, hoping that all would be well.

DAY 154

DAY 155

In the middle of our transition chaos, a small news story caught my attention. A little boy and his sister had been hit by a car while waiting to cross the street with their mother. It had been broad daylight at a marked crosswalk, and they had been waiting on the sidewalk. I had read about other tragedies in the days and weeks before, but for some reason, this story struck me in the heart.

I dreamed of the mother and her two children. I wondered how they were and whether the little boy, who had sustained the most severe injuries, would be okay. I cried for this family that I didn't know and I held them in my heart. And then, while visiting a friend, I discovered that the boy and his sister went to the same school my children had attended before homeschooling, and that they were known to our friends. Suddenly the reason why this felt close made sense.

DAY
156

DAY
157

*This one is of the lavender inclination.
She is tiny (of course!) and sweet and very
mellow. She will surely bring tranquility
to the world — she already does...*

As news spread, our community organized to bring dinners to the family while they waited for their son to grow strong and well again. The sister and mother had both recovered, but the boy was so badly injured that no one was sure what to expect when he woke up. I was anguished that I could not participate; we were deep into the packing phase and often eating out of cans. I decided that though I couldn't make the family food, I could make the boy a gnome — a little gnome that might bring a smile or a bit of hope, a little someone to watch over him and wait with his family. And so I did. I thought of a boy I had never seen, and his mother, and how heavy her heart must be in the face of her child's injuries, and I felted. I sent the gnome with a friend and told her to let them know that I thought of them and that this gnome was made just for their little boy and their family. She took it with her, along with the meals, cards, thoughts, and prayers.

DAY

164

DAY

163

DAY 168

DAY 167

DAY 166

173

Later, I got an email, a little message from that same friend who had delivered the well wishes and gifts. "He spoke for the first time today. He said his first word since the accident," she wrote in her email. "He said 'gnome.'"

I cried long and hard at that. Even if no one else thought a thing about those gnomes — wool and a pipe cleaner felted into a little person — one boy, with a long road of healing ahead, had brightened at the sight of one. It wasn't a cure for cancer, it wasn't a species saved, but it was something. And that was enough.

I kept making gnomes.

12

Children, Dogs, Guinea Pigs and a Cat

hen it came time to decide what would go in our minivan for the epic cross-country haul, Jens and I argued about the wool.

"You can't have your felting kit. It's too big," he said, looking at the leather tote on wheels my mother had found at a thrift store during her March visit. It was about sixteen inches in height and width and about eight inches deep, hardly a monolith. But it allowed me to fit a pound and a half of wool, several felting tools, extra needles, and pipe cleaners all into one portable space.

DAY
177

I'd like to report that I used eloquent and calm words to persuade him to compromise, but that would be a bald-faced lie. Instead I felt my temper rise, and a good kick of adrenaline coursed through me at the mere thought of not having my kit at the ready. I'm sure my voice held a note of hysteria as I screeched, "You have got to be *kidding* me! I didn't make one gnome a day all this time only to stop because we're moving our lives across the country in an overcrowded minivan. Oh no, buddy, if you think I'm going to stop now, then you've got another thing coming. Leave something of yours behind. *The kit stays.*"

Smart man that he is, he backed off and nodded, designating an area in the back for what had become my kit of sanity.

DAY

183

DAY

180

DAY
187

DAY
190

DAY
188

DAY
189

DAY
191

This gnome made me think about the Pacific NW forests — the ferns and moss and the way you get these little purple surprise flowers sometimes and the way the cedar and redwood bark is nice and reddish. So, this gnome — he's all about the forest and the secret lovely surprises there.

There was a little voice in my head that asked why I was so protective of these gnomes. After all, it would be understandable if I didn't make them while we were in transition. But it wouldn't be one gnome; it would be pretty much a week's worth that I would not have made if I used the move as an excuse. And we were driving. Driving almost four thousand miles. I was going to need something to do. So, after packing the children, animals, food, clothing, and household items into the van, I pulled enough wool and supplies out of the kit to make a gnome en route that first day of travel.

Trekking across the country is no small task, and it's even more complicated with four children, two dogs, a cat, and two guinea pigs. The cat and guinea pigs were in two separate crates, stacked one on top of the other in the middle of the backseat, with the eight-year-old on one side and the ten-year-old on the other to calm them. While the dogs wedged and re-wedged themselves into various inches of floor space throughout the trip, I kept my wool out of their sniff zone. I had learned the hard way years before that felted wool items held a substantial allure for dogs. Something about the smell of wool (perhaps

CHILDREN, DOGS, GUINEA PIGS AND A CAT

they picked up "eau de sheep" even when it was not noticeable to humans) inspired dogs to mouth, rip apart, and all too often completely devour wool art pieces. I knew I wouldn't handle it well if one of the road trip gnomes ended up headless. Or worse.

Originally we thought that by driving, we could see the country and have one of those long-ago road trips frequently taken by families of yesteryear. I had delusions of singing and storytelling, all sunshine, buttercups, and unicorns as we looked at the Grand Canyon and gasped at the grand expanse of the Mississippi River.

There were definitely good memories made, the ones that you sit back and think about later and smile; but our journey did not take us to the Grand Canyon or the Mississippi, and there weren't any unicorns. We drove through the middle of the country, which, in case you haven't had the pleasure, is remarkably flat when you aren't in the mountains and is, without a doubt, incredibly beautiful but can be swelteringly hot in the summer.

We made space to see Mount Rushmore and Crazy Horse, both of which are outstanding and almost surreal in their grandeur. And as I sat in the passenger seat, I made gnomes through Idaho, Utah, Wyoming, Colorado, and the Dakotas. I made

a gnome on the day we saw both of the historic monuments, and more gnomes as we drove through cities and across majestic plains.

There was one night when I didn't manage, when the very idea of lifting my finger in the name of anything felt far too overwhelming. It was the first time I said the words, "I am not making a gnome tonight. I'm choosing not to."

It had been a long day. I'm not sure whether it was the day after I slept next to the toilet in the too-small motel room to keep the cat company so she would be quiet. Or whether it was the day the cat pooped in her crate and we had to pull over in the middle of nowhere to clean things up. Or whether it was the day the children fought viciously across the aisle like Congress over a bill — neither side willing to give an inch. But it was one of those days, and when we arrived at our motel it was 11:30 p.m. and we had been in the car since 6 a.m. I looked at my kit and turned to the children and Jens and said, "Not tonight. I'm taking the day off." I went to bed, hoping to grab six hours of sleep before we did it all again.

The decision was perhaps one of my most deeply experienced moments of the year, that moment when I consciously chose not to. Even as I spoke the words, I felt the disappointment and letdown of that incomplete day. The next day, there was an uncomfortable sensation that I had failed — not the project, but myself. I had chosen not to do this one simple task. I wasn't sick and I hadn't forgotten; I just didn't do it. That's when I realized that the act of gnoming every day had embedded in me a sense of purpose. It was my PB&J, and having skipped it consciously I had stepped out of the one thing that held a solid piece of rhythm in my life. I had *willingly* given it up.

The freedom that I had imagined was eluding me because I had committed to this one strange small practice was nothing more than a figment of my imagination. I was startled to discover that satisfaction didn't come in having chosen not to do something, but in the very opposite. Making a gnome was the one thing guaranteed to bring fulfillment. At the end of every day, even if everything had fallen apart, or things had gone wrong or had felt unsatisfactory, I could look down at that little woolen elemental and smile at the one small thing I *had* accomplished.

The absence of Gnome #205 served as a marker for me. It would never be so easy to choose not to do something again.

Turning
Inside Out

*M*oving is one of those things that can turn you inside out. It can be new and exciting and magical right from the start and ever after, or it can be new and exciting and magical and then it can wane and leave you lost. The latter is how it was for me. Having lived my entire adult life in and near a city of strong diversity and kinship, moving to a tiny town where things were so very different threw me. Hard.

When Jens returned to his job on the West Coast until he could join us permanently in December, I was alone with the children for the first time in my life. I still made gnomes, but these gnomes were an anchor. They were what tied me to the life I'd had before, a life that I knew and understood and loved, while I learned to swim in these new waters.

The weather was warm and dreamy and the people were kind and welcoming. The children played in the river and threw the ball for our dogs. We played in fields and traipsed through the forest and looked at moss beds in search of elves and fairies. Yet I still did not feel at home. The very air was foreign, and each breath brought with it excitement for and fear of the newness of this place — the dialect, the lifestyle, the philosophies, and even the grocery store were so different from what I had known that all of it added to

DAY
221

DAY
218

the ache for something familiar growing in my heart. I walked the rooms of the old home we had adopted and dreamed of how it would be when the messy, unfinished mud jobs were fixed and the failing plaster was replaced. I explored the wonky rooms and admired the dip in the stair treads where countless feet of different sizes had stepped on their way up and down the grand staircase. But something seemed to be missing.

So I made gnomes. I made them outside and inside. I made them at night and during the day. I made them while laughing about antics cooked up by the children and while crying about the lack of community and close friends. And every time I made one, there was a little spark of contentment, a little voice inside that said, *This is you and you are doing something. Even if it won't win you a peace prize or change the world, it is changing you and you are part of this world.*

The transition from one coast to another, one culture to another, one tribe to another, a small house to a big house, a milder climate to a cold and severe one — all of that challenged me more than almost any other transition in my life. And my one salvation was my daily gnome.

While the children explored the river with the dogs, I stood watch and hung laundry. We looked up at the stars at night and listened to the bats singing to us from behind the siding, and we imagined the goats, chickens, ducks, and geese in their farmyard, where we hoped they would be frolicking by the following summer. We built bonfires in the fire pit, and neighborhood children brought hot dogs and whooped as they fed the fire and felt powerful. Things were so beautiful but so different from what I expected, and I struggled to marry my dreams to reality. Back in Oregon, I had

DAY **227**

DAY **229**

DAY **234**

flipped through photographs of our Maine home and imagined a house full of color and life with new friends dropping in to visit. I had envisioned a yard wild with gardens. Instead, I found that I was lonely for someone to share tea and conversation with. The yard was large, and, having no green thumb, I wasn't sure what to plant, where to put it, or how to make sure it survived the winter. And though I could wield a paintbrush, I couldn't fix or build like Jens. A distinct sense of disappointment that I could not move faster toward our goals began to take hold of me.

DAY
239

DAY
240

September came along, and the children started school. Though we had planned to homeschool, the schools here were well-funded and offered a plethora of subjects and activities, and the children were champing at the bit. When the bus drove away that first morning, I looked around and wondered what on earth I was going to do. I was alone . . . echo, echo, echo, echo. Yes, that alone. So I made gnomes. This fellow was made this afternoon — with sunshine pouring from the windows.

Things only got harder. The children, sensing my struggle, began to struggle more themselves, especially without a mother who could provide the rhythm and steadiness necessary to keep things in balance. I was just trying to keep my head above water. Jens was far away and helpless. I tried to keep a brave face and failed most of the time. The well ran dry if we did more than one load of laundry or if we took a shower longer than five minutes, and we got really good at washing dishes with minimal water.

DAY
244

DAY
252

DAY
248

One night, upon returning from a school event, we discovered that our boxer mix had encountered a skunk and proceeded to rub her face on every fabric-covered object in the house in an effort to rid herself of the stench. The pillows from my grandmother, the new couch (a gift from my mother), and all, count them, *five beds* were completely covered in the same smell. It was a long night.

DAY 262

DAY 260

But I needed to put it behind me, so naturally I made gnomes. Even when I felt I couldn't do anything right or get anything done, I made a gnome.

DAY 263

DAY 264

DAY 266

Skunked

I *continued to hope for* peace of mind in Maine. Remembering how streetlamps in Portland lit up the sky, reducing our ability to see the true scope of the stars, I sought out those celestial bodies every night. They reminded me that I had been granted an endless night sky, even if nothing else seemed to be quite what I expected. I had also hoped for an ally or two as well as inspiration to start writing, or a sudden muse for art outside of the daily gnome, but I felt vacant. I had turned myself inside out to make this move, but now I was certain that it was only going to get harder, darker, and more difficult before things got better — if they ever did. The sense that I had lost my tribe, and with it a piece of myself, pervaded my life, and I couldn't help but wonder: What if this was all wrong? What if I was fooling myself into thinking that we were supposed to be anywhere but in our cottage in Oregon, where we knew who we were and what we were doing in life?

DAY
267

DAY
268

DAY
269

DAY
270

THE *gnome* PROJECT

Relief finally came in the form of Jens flying in to take up the broom and dishcloth and give me a break. He was originally supposed to stay only three days, but he saw the writing on the wall, so he surprised me by making it a full week.

It was a week of "Daddy, look what I learned!" and "Poppa, in school I have a friend who likes drawing just like me!" And I got to sleep in. It was glorious, and for a moment I could see how life could be and would be soon. In a couple of months, I would have another adult, one who knew me well, to help carry the load and check in with at the end of the day. When it came time for him to go, I turned into a puddle and he tearfully packed his suitcase for the bus trip to Boston and subsequent flight back to Oregon. I dreaded the return to my solitary parenting journey.

DAY
273

SKUNKED

123

It was at this point that the parade of skunks re-sumed. One paid a visit to our furry family members on my daughter's thirteenth birthday, shortly before we headed out to dinner. And though that was a nasty fiasco, it was the third run-in the following day that resulted in the worst of our skunky disasters. My mother, up for a visit, and I had walked down to the river to marvel at it that afternoon, and our boxer mix had gone off into the dry leaves, sniffing.

It couldn't have been more than a moment or two before she was growling and then barking furiously, and we turned to see a skunk hanging from her face, attached firmly to nose and lip. I screamed, Mother shouted, and our golden retriever stood nearby wagging her tail, unwilling to engage but not wishing to miss a single moment. I stood back shouting, "Leave it! *Leave it!*" To no avail. Three minutes later, the skunk was dead, the boxer bloodied but triumphant, and the golden was still wagging away.

Calls were placed to animal control and the veterinarian, and hysteria made its way through me as they explained that both my dogs, though vaccinated, would need to be quarantined until the skunk's carcass could be tested and cleared of rabies.

DAY
277

SKUNKED

In retrospect, I am surprised that I didn't throw in the towel and move back to Oregon that very day, or go to bed with a bottle of wine and stay there, but I had to keep going. The curse of being the only parent on the premises was also the blessing that kept me chugging away, even when all I wanted was to assume the fetal position. I packed all my wool paintings and gnomes away to shield them from what I was certain would be the permanent odor of my new home and tried to figure out how to make a gnome without him getting skunked in the process.

That's when I changed tactics. Instead of damning the skunk as I had the first two times, I wanted to know *why*. Why was I running up against this stinky creature over and over again? The locals were getting a good laugh and the animal control officer told me that he didn't know anyone who'd had as many nasty encounters with skunks as I'd experienced in recent history. There had to be a reason. I didn't know where to turn to fix this or even to ask the question. After all, to most of the people in town, I was that crazy woman from "away" who made gnomes. And then I ran into our kind neighbor Nancy.

Nancy had started to blossom into a new friend, and when she dropped by one day and saw how upset I was, she suggested I see her friend Dana, a visiting intuitive who was coming to town to do readings. The idea seemed silly, but on my way home a few days later, I found myself pulling into Nancy's driveway. What could it hurt?

I found the two women in the backyard. Nancy turned to Dana and said, "Jessica has a skunk problem. Tell her, Jessica." Dana looked nothing like I imagined. I had envisioned a willowy, pristinely dressed woman in flowing garments, emanating wisdom with an all-knowing countenance — a female version of Gandalf the Grey. This woman was

jean-clad and wearing a flannel shirt, with steely, piercing eyes and a cigarette in her hand. When she looked at me, I got a distinct and unsettling impression that she saw far more in people than she would ever let on, and that it was something that weighed heavily on her.

I told her about the three incidents and my fear of rabies exposure. I told her about my dogs, depressed and cooped up in crates in the house, and all my wool and gnomes tucked away to protect them from the onslaught of constant odor. I mentioned that my husband was still in Oregon and wouldn't be joining us for months yet and that I was facing this skunk issue (and any others that arose) alone.

She listened, and then looked at me with those penetrating eyes and shook her head. Her voice was raspy. "First off, you're the one who's been giving me a stomachache. I've been telling Nancy all day that someone was in a bad way around here, and then you drove up and it got worse." She stopped and took a drag off her cigarette.

"What I'm getting from this skunk thing is pretty straightforward. The skunk is trying to tell you, quite literally, that 'This stinks.' You need to fix whatever it is that is out of balance. Go fix things and it will stop."

"Like what?" I asked, hoping for some sort of pointer.

She shook her head. "You have to figure it out. I just tell you what I see."

I went home, sprinkled cinnamon on the rugs again, lit incense, and asked myself, over and over again, *What is out of balance?* Eventually, I pulled out some gnome-making supplies and got to work meditating on the question between the *chk chk chk*s of the needle.

As the days passed, I began to piece together an answer. I noticed that though I tried to focus on the positives of the move — like that starry night sky — most of the time I was far more focused on the ways it wasn't living up to my expectations. I paid more attention to what I didn't have — a partner to share the load with, a garden to harvest food from, the farm animals I'd dreamed of for so many years — than on the things I did have: a beautiful old house that was unique and welcoming where my children could run themselves ragged, kind and generous neighbors who showered us with ripe vegetables from their own abundant gardens, and two dogs, two guinea pigs, and a cat who kept us company through our days.

I began to strive with consciousness to find a place of gratitude, always seeking out the hidden thank-yous in my days. It was by no means an overnight transformation, and I don't know how deep and valid Dana's powers of intuition were, but I will tell you this: The skunks started leaving us alone. Sure, it could have been because my overly enthusiastic boxer had put an end to the problem. Yet I wasn't quite willing to write off the other possibility: that I had begun to find equilibrium. Life got a little brighter, and I furthered my efforts to find positivity, wrapping its fine, silver strands around my soul like a cloak to ward off the dark I had almost let consume me.

DAY 288

SKUNKED

Finding the
Flip Side

As I cultivated gratitude, I began to understand that I was right where I was supposed to be: in Maine, in a town of a thousand people, in a grand old battered house a five-hour drive from my mother. But I didn't know why I felt so sure of that. And I didn't know what I was supposed to be doing now that I was there.

Until I figured it out, I decided I had better start looking for work before our bank account ran dry. I had not fully considered the consequences that being rural would have on my small art and teaching business, so I submitted applications for as many jobs as I could find around the area. I applied for bank teller and bookkeeping positions, telemarketing operator and waitressing jobs. Within a week, I was hired by a large sandwich chain and put to work part-time. I came home smelling like baked bread and cold cuts, but I had a paycheck and that was something.

I made gnomes at night, one by one at the end of long days full of so much newness that I thought I would go crazy from it. The gnomes kept me intact like that PB&J. As everything else around me changed, I had the gnomes. At least they remained the same.

In my quest to find follow-through, I found that the treasure of a daily practice isn't just in the act itself but in the underlying knowledge that you are accomplishing something and you are anchored. It is in the knowledge that comes on small, quiet feet to let you know you are capable. It is in the feeling of having found something that creates a shift inside you without you having to do anything besides practice.

My diligence in the making of these small creatures was steadfast, and on the rare days that I skipped, I felt less remorse. I worked my odd and sometimes erratic schedule; I took care of the children, shuttling them to their various school activities and playdates; and I felt gnomes.

A Welcomed Part
of the Day

he original plan was that Jens would join us in mid-December, but being divided by so much distance was taking its toll, so he came early, joining us shortly before Thanksgiving. The drive was grueling. At times he had to pull over, unable to see past the flying snow, his windshield wipers frozen to the glass. I tracked his progress, hiding it from the children, hoping to surprise them with his early arrival. And then he was home. For three months, I had been doing the single-mom thing — not long in the scheme of things, not an Olympic feat by any stretch, but it was hard and I had done it. The children had eaten more mac and cheese than I would ever feed them again, and we had spent more evenings than I wished to admit watching Britcoms, but I had made it through. I had played the part of two parents, made connections for my business, gotten a job, painted four rooms in the house, managed to get children to soccer games, gotten to know some of my neighbors — and I had made gnomes.

With Jens finally on the same coast, I was relieved of some of the transportation and household duties. He spent his days weatherizing the home, finding the many holes that gave way to every little breeze as the temperature dropped, and searching for jobs. A stellar résumé and rock-star recommendations from every single boss he'd worked for over the last twenty-five years were sent out over and over again. Meanwhile, I made sandwiches, tried to keep up with the enormity of such a giant house, and made gnomes. Always those gnomes.

There were bad days when I didn't make a gnome because I was too tired or feeling ill, and a couple of times when I was actually ill, but I didn't ream myself. I just woke up the next day and resolved not to miss *that* day and *that* gnome.

When I took a moment to explore why I wasn't beating myself up about the lapses, I discovered that what had been an effort and a force of will to accomplish, what I had thought of as unattainable, had become a breath, a heartbeat, a part of my being. When I missed a day, it wasn't that I was stopping; it was simply that I had missed a day. I still felt the strangeness in having missed a gnome, but I wasn't cruel to myself about it.

Though in the beginning, I tagged and kept close track of the gnomes, by November I had mixed up several batches. I lapsed in photo taking, and I had to list many of them later as "date unknown." I admit to giving myself a bit of a talking-to: "You could take the time to tag them. That isn't too hard."

My only defense was that the daily practice was to *make* a gnome, not tag it and list it, and by not tracking and still making them every day, it had become organic and natural.

My children would ask, "Hey, Mom, did you make your gnome yet today?"

Somehow, the gnomes had integrated into our lives. They were expected and welcomed as part of the day. I just hoped that the side effect would be that since I had so many, I would be able to sell them during the holidays. With money tight, most people in our area flocked to big-box stores for gifts, so the "Buy Local" mantra that was celebrated and revered in Portland was expensive and luxurious here. The gnomes accumulated.

Or Jens would check in and say, "Why don't we listen to a story and you can make a gnome?"

One ever-supportive customer planned to adorn her tree with them and gave them to everyone she knew, reminding me periodically of the magic of these gnomes. With her enthusiasm and my mother's ever-present words of encouragement echoing in my head, I took a leap and went in for a jury appointment at an art center that sold selected works by local artists.

They weren't in the jury room long before they came back out to invite me in to talk further about my product. Two days later, a gallery called and took sixty gnomes on commission, and two weeks after that, the art center emailed my acceptance. Acceptance didn't necessarily mean that they would order right away, and so close to Christmas I didn't hold out much hope, but they did order and gnomes were delivered.

All the
Difference

ecember promised my mother's much-awaited visit for the holidays. For the first time in many years, we would be able to spend Christmas with her, and the children were ecstatic. Every year something had come up or plans had fallen apart, but not this time. On the day she arrived, I made a gnome — no surprise there — and every night during her magical visit, we sat down on the couch and talked or watched a movie while I made a gnome.

The gnomes that remained after the art center and gallery had taken their orders began to sell online. Although I wanted the income, the rhythm of making the gnomes was far more sustainable than the photographing and listing of them. Soon they began to accumulate in the inventory box again.

My mother left the day before New Year's Eve, and I started to come down from the holiday out-breath. Jens

found temporary work, and the children went back to school. One day just barely into the new year, I found myself alone on a rare day off. In a sudden rush of purpose and financial responsibility, I pulled out the box of gnomes to start the process of listing them online.

What I found shocked me. Once they were laid out, awaiting their chance in front of the camera, there were almost twenty of them.

Many days had gone by and each one had a gnome. I hadn't skipped any of them. I hadn't tagged them, so I didn't know which one went with which day, but I did photograph them and then I went to the blog.

I scrolled down and looked through the past entries. Hundreds of gnomes were looking back at me, and each one stood for a day in a year of my life. And not just any year, a big year, a year so full of change that I still don't know how it all fit into 366 days. Normally when I look at a year, I think, *Wait, what happened in May? When did we go camping?* But this year, this epically awaited year, was measured in gnomes. They told me my story. They reminded me of what happened each day and helped me follow my footprints back to landmarks along the way.

As the months wore on, making these gnomes went far beyond a daily practice. They became a symbol of hope. I found that not only had I evolved, but I had used my own unique brand of willpower to make more than 366 gnomes. I had grown as a person before my very eyes, and I was proud of myself. And all of this was done with wool, pipe cleaners, a felting needle, and my own two hands.

These gnomes were a reflection of an entire year and season in my life, and I had stayed with them through all of it. And, quite remarkably, I discovered that they had stayed with me. The gnomes gave me confidence and prompted an evolution of character. These gnomes gave me back to myself.

I'm not perfect. I haven't become the most diligent person — focused and steadfast at follow-through — but I'm getting better at it and I *believe* that I can do it, and that makes all the difference. Sometimes it takes something small and seemingly innocuous or silly to catapult us further into our quest to become better people.

Mary Oliver wrote: "Tell me, what is it you plan to do with your one wild and precious life?"

To that I can only say I'm not entirely sure. But for a year of *my* wild and precious life, I made gnomes — little wool gnomes with pointed hats and impish faces and the surprising power to awaken deep change. I made them one at a time. And now, as I breathe in and out, I celebrate the rhythm of my days and find peace in a life I have learned to call home.

Postscript

The project was to make one gnome a day for a year, but at the end of that year, I decided to take it a step farther and not make a gnome a day for a year. I felt that I wouldn't reach completion until I knew not only what it was like to have a daily practice, but what it was like not to have it. That year was 2013. I have since weighed my options and have loved how much I remember of 2012 and how much more relaxed and complete my life felt with the solidity of a gnome daily practice. So on January 1, 2014, I started up the gnome-a-day project again, and it is really nice to be making them again with such regularity: one by one, day by day. Once again my days are measured in gnomes, which apparently is going to be the currency of my life — at least for now. I encourage you to go out into this dynamic, beautiful world of ours and find something that challenges you — in a good way — then strive to create your own daily practice and see what unfolds in your heart and in your life. You are capable, even when you think you aren't. Take it from me.

How to Make a Gnome

$\mathcal{S}$*ince I love needle felting so much,* I wanted to share that love and I began teaching classes. Yes, I've been cursed by people who, after learning to needle felt, looked at me, shook their heads, and said, "I didn't need anything else to love in my life that I don't have time for. Thanks a lot."

I can't help it. The world needs art. It needs fewer people using the words *I'm not an artist* or *I'm not artistic*, and more people indulging in the necessity of making art and letting it become whatever it is. That *is* art.

As with any new project, take your time and enjoy the journey. Make sure you do the steps as you read them. Don't try to guess what part of the pipe cleaner will end up as which part of the gnome or things might get a little tangled. Gnomes will surprise you, so take it one step at a time and you'll get there. Let's get started.

Supplies

- *1 regular-size piped cleaner*

- *¼ ounce of wool roving in the skin tone color of your choice*

- *¼ ounce of wool roving in the pant color of your choice*

- *¼ ounce of wool roving in the shirt color of your choice*

- *¼ ounce of wool roving in the hat color of your choice*

- *A handful of wool roving for the beard color of your choice*

- *A little bit of black wool roving for the eyes*

- *1 foam felting pad*

- *1 #38 fine felting needle (you will probably want extras; breaking needles in the beginning is not uncommon)*

- *1 five-needle felting tool (optional!)*

Felting Tips

If you have never felted before, there are things you should keep in mind.

It is only the very end of the needle that does the felting, so you don't have to stick the whole needle in to get results. Also, because of sewing and knitting and crocheting, we are more used to using a dipping motion or a twisting motion. You can't dip, dig, or twist with a felting needle. You need to remember to go straight in and straight out to avoid breaking off the tip. Needles will break, of course, but if it happens a lot, watch your technique and see what may be causing it.

Just because you are poking straight in and out doesn't mean you can't do straight pokes from different angles. Angles are awfully handy when felting.

Felting needles hurt! Keep Band-Aids nearby and go slowly. Just as sewing can cause some pokes and pain, so can needle felting, so use caution. I can't even count how many times I have stabbed myself.

Felting pads are necessary. I use high-density foam pads that are usually 3½ to 4 inches thick, though you can use 2-inch-thick pads as well. Remember to use the pad on a hard surface and not on your lap. I have been known to stab my leg through my project and through the foam. It is a painful experience that I do not recommend.

Making the Head

1   The first thing to do is take your chosen
    skin tone (hereafter called "skin wool"; yes,
    it's sort of morbid), tear a strip 12 inches
    long and 1 inch wide (when flattened out),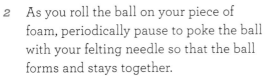
    and begin to roll it into a tight little ball
    as if you were winding yarn. You will
    probably end up turning and pinching the
    wool repeatedly to shape it.

2   As you roll the ball on your piece of
    foam, periodically pause to poke the ball
    with your felting needle so that the ball
    forms and stays together.

3   Leave a tail so it looks like a comet, and
    stop when the head is slightly bigger
    than a quarter. Felt it up nice and tight
    by poking it quite a bit with the needle,
    turning the ball to keep it round. Tear
    off any excess wool on the tail so the tail
    measures about 3 inches.

4   Decide which side will be the face and
    indent a straight horizontal line across
    the middle, using the needle to poke
    the head. This is your eye line.

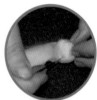

5   Take a small tuft of skin wool for the
    nose. Using the same rolling technique
    you used for the head, make a tiny ball.
    It doesn't have to be tightly felted.

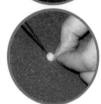

6   Position the nose in the center just
    below the eye line and poke it around
    the edges very carefully to attach it
    firmly to the face.

7   Next, choose a small amount of skin
    wool, tear it up a bit, and then flatten it
    out to create a thin veil slightly larger
    than the head. The veil will be about
    2 inches by 3 inches.

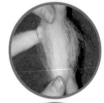

8   Place this thin layer over the face and
    nose. Carefully tack it around the edges
    past the hairline. Felt the edges of the
    veil onto the back of the head.

9   Using the #38 fine needle, felt the veil onto the face, poking around the nose and on the cheeks and forehead. This creates a better finish on the gnome's face.

10 Once you feel satisfied with the attachment and smoothness, you can choose where you want the eyes and, using the same #38 needle, indent holes on either side of the nose, on the eye line.

11 I poke the same spot repeatedly until it indents to my liking. Now your gnome has a head.

Making the Body

Take your pipe cleaner and carefully bend each tip down tightly against itself to create a blunt end. Only bend over the very ends or your gnome will be too small. Now you're ready to make the body.

1   Tear a piece of skin wool about 12 inches long and ¼ inch wide (when flattened, like a ribbon). Start about ¾ inch from one end of the pipe cleaner. This will be your gnome's leg and the starting point for the entire body. Hold the tail of the wool and wrap, flattening the wool as if it were ribbon so that there are no twists or lumps around the pipe cleaner. (That said, if it does lump, don't worry. You'll get better as you make more!) Wrap the ¾-inch section to the end of the pipe cleaner, leaving a tail.

2   Once you reach the end of the pipe cleaner, bend ¼ inch of the newly wrapped pipe cleaner end back up on itself so it looks like a small U. Squeeze that U as tightly possible to make it thin.

3   Then wrap the tail of skin wool over the wool-wrapped U. Keep wrapping until you are about 1½ inches up the pipe cleaner. You now have your first leg and foot. If you have excess wool, use your felting needle to felt the wool a little (be careful of the pipe cleaner; you don't want to break your needle in the wires that run through it) and tear off the excess.

4   Measure from your newly wrapped foot up about 2 inches to where you probably stopped wrapping and bend the pipe cleaner into an upside-down V. That point in the V is the crotch of the gnome. The longer side of the V is what you will use to make the second leg, torso, and arms.

5   The second leg is the next step. Starting at the point of the V, measure down until you find the point on the long side that is equal in length to the first gnome leg you wrapped. When you find that point, go ahead and bend the pipe cleaner there. Now your V looks more like an N.

6   Take a strip of skin roving about 12 inches long and ¼ inch wide — the same size, thickness, and width as the one you used to make the first leg. Starting ¾ inch above the new bend you put in the pipe cleaner, hold the very end of the roving and wrap it down toward the bend. Wrap the pipe cleaner around the bend you made and then back up the other side of the bend as if you were going to wrap the rest of the pipe cleaner. Remember to keep the wool flat like a ribbon and avoid twists and lumps as you go. Stop when you get about ½ inch past the bend in the pipe cleaner. Be sure to leave a tail of about 4 inches long.

7   The newly wrapped area will be similar to the U you made with the first foot.

8   Press the U together tightly to make it thin. Take the tail of skin wool and wrap it around both sides of the U, covering them. You will have something that looks like an upside-down Y.

The unwrapped pipe cleaner (the tail of the Y) is what you will use for the body and arms. There should be more than half of the pipe cleaner left. If you have excess wool, use your felting needle to felt the wool a little (again, be careful so you don't break your needle on the pipe cleaner) and tear off the excess.

9   Now that you have feet and legs, it's time to make the arms. Take the tail of the Y and bend it down to measure it against one of the gnome's legs. I like to make the arms the same length as the legs.

10 When you have the unwrapped pipe-cleaner section lined up, bend it just like you did when you were making the feet. Create that U shape to mark it. Open the little U and, taking a strip of your skin wool about 12 inches long and ¼ inch wide (the same dimensions as you used for the feet), start wrapping about ¾ inch above the bend on one side of the U, then wrap down toward the bend.

11 Wrap around the bend and back up the other side for ½ inch.

12 Stop wrapping, press both sides of the new U together, and use the tail of skin wool to wrap around the U the same way you did for the feet, only this time you are making a hand. If you have excess wool, use your felting needle to felt the wool a little (careful of the pipe cleaner) and tear off the excess.

13 Now you have your first arm. The rest of the pipe cleaner will create the second arm.

14 Measure the second arm against the leg on that side; use your best judgment to decide if everything looks even enough. Bend the remaining section of pipe cleaner down to measure it against the toe and then bend it into the U shape.

15 Use a piece of skin wool about 12 inches long and ¼ inch wide, similar in size to those you used for the feet and the first

hand, and wrap down toward the bend and then back up the other side of the bend.

16 Stop. Use the tail to wrap both sides of the U together.

17 You have now finished the second arm and the body, and the wool roving should completely cover the pipe cleaner. If you have excess wool, use your felting needle to felt it a little (careful of the pipe cleaner). Tear off the excess.

Attaching the Head to the Body

Remember the tail on your gnome's head? Remember how it looks kind of like a comet? That comet tail is how you will attach the head to the body.

1. First, split the comet tail in two, carefully. Then place the head on the arms, in the center.

2. Using the two tails, wrap diagonally in opposite directions under the arm and over the opposite shoulder to create an X. I do this one at a time at first and then take turns — like lacing shoes — to create evenness. I wrap the tails around the neck a couple of times, too.

3. Your head is now attached. You will need to pull out your needle and carefully felt all the way around the neck to make sure it is solidly in place. Again, remember to use caution. Felting needles get caught between the wires that wind around each other in the center of a pipe cleaner and can break.

Dressing the Gnome: The Pants

I always start with the pants. I don't know why, but I do. If you need to reposition the arms and legs to maneuver the clothing wool, go ahead and do that. You can always bend them back into place later.

1   Take your pant wool and tear a strip about 12 inches long and ½ inch wide. You can play around with thickness, but remember to wrap it like ribbon — flat. Wrap it around your gnome's waist.

2   Wrap the wool down his leg to where his ankle would be and stop.

3   Wrap it around his ankle area once or twice and then wrap it back up his leg to the waist. If you don't think the pants are thick enough, you can add more layers using the same technique. If you run out of pant wool, add another strip.

4   Once the pant leg looks right to you, start wrapping the second leg.

5   When you're finished with both pant legs, end by wrapping the excess around the waist several times. If you run out of pant wool strip before you are done, start at the waist and keep wrapping until it seems right.

6   Use your felting needle to poke the pants all over to firm them up. This is important — they might unravel if you skip this step.

Dressing the Gnome: The Shirt

The process of creating the shirt is similar to the one used to create the pants.

1   Tear strips of your shirt wool and wrap the arms, starting at the waist the way you did with the pants. Wrap up the torso, down the arm toward the wrist, and then back up toward the torso.

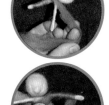

2   I needle felt gently as I go. I use the shirt wool to create the stomach, and I like to wrap extra shirt wool around the waist to thicken it up a bit.

3   Wrap the shirt wool around the neck, across the shoulder to the opposite armpit, and back around the waist.

4   Repeat the wrapping down to the wrist and back up to the torso on each arm.

5   Wrap around the waist and neck
    to stabilize everything and keep it
    even.

6   You will want that felting needle
    to firm up the stomach and arms,
    especially the stomach — gnomes
    tend to be rather jolly-bellied folk,
    and you want them to have solid
    bellies. If you have extra shirt wool
    hanging off, go ahead and tear it off
    once you have firmed up the wool
    with the felting needle.

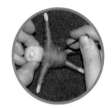

7   To make the feet, bend the ¼ inch at
    the bottom of each leg to a 90-degree
    angle.

8   With the pants and shirt done, you
    are in the home stretch: the hat,
    beard, and eyes!

Dressing the Gnome: The Hat

This is a very important piece. Without the hat, your gnome isn't quite gnomish enough. Legend has it that they only take their hats off to sleep, at which point they most likely look like very, very small people.

1   Choose a strip of hat wool about 10 or 12 inches by 1½ inches wide (when flattened) and press it out a bit. Spread the fibers out so that it is flatter but not thin or sheer. Then start to roll it like you might roll up a rug, but place your thumb in one end to create an indent as you roll. This is where it will go on the gnome's head.

2   You don't want it to be uniform like a hot dog, so you want to roll it at an angle so that it begins to look cone-ish.

3   Once you have a decent cone, pull out that needle and start poking. Don't forget to remove your thumb. If the hat is the shape and size you want, but you still have hat wool hanging off the cone,

felt the hat up a bit so it holds and tear off the extra wool. You want to poke it enough for it to stay in a cone shape. Rotate the cone as you poke it so that it doesn't flatten into a shape that won't fit on your gnome's head. Felt it up firmly, but leave the edge where you had your thumb less felted so the fibers there can be felted into the head.

4   Place the hat on the gnome's head and start felting the edge. You may need to hold it down and work in one area to anchor it before making your way around the head. Keep poking and moving around the head. Often this is the part that takes the longest. You want that hat very well attached, so take your time.

5   Poke the back of the neck and the hairline, and then poke where the hat covers the head, firmly attaching it.

6   Clean up the hairline with slow, careful pokes when you are comfortable with the firmness of the attachment.

7   At this point, I tear a strip of hat wool that is about ½ inch wide and long enough to go around the head twice. I anchor it with felting to the back of the neck and then carefully encircle the hairline twice, felting it as I go. You may want to go back over the hairline and redefine it by carefully poking the needle where the hat meets the head so the hat doesn't look like it is fading into the gnome's head.

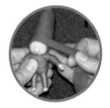

Dressing the Gnome:
The Beard

The beard is pretty straightforward.

1   Take some of your beard wool and tear it
    up a bit.

2   Lay the beard on the gnome's face just
    below the nose and where the ears would
    be, and begin poking. I use many tufts
    that I attach one at a time, blending as
    I go, and build up until I am satisfied.

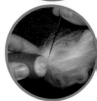

3   You can then add bangs if you would like.

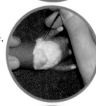

4   I like to add hair at the edge of the hat
    on the back of the neck, for stability as
    well as continuity with the beard.

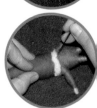

The Eyes

I leave the eyes for last. It just doesn't feel right for something to have eyes while its body is disassembled and you are stabbing things into it, you know?

1   Using the tiny tuft of eye wool and your needle, poke the tuft into the indented eyeholes/sockets you created when you made your head. You don't need to shape the wool; simply poke it in the eye socket indent until it's the size and shape you wish it to be. Sometimes an eye needs only a tiny wisp of wool, and sometimes it needs more; it is about what size eye you want and how densely you felted your head.

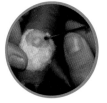

2   Delicately poke the wool into the sockets, and you have eyes.

Congratulations, you just finished your first gnome! It will get easier with every gnome, so roll up those sleeves and make some more!

Gnome-Making Variations: Making a Skirt

1   To make a girl gnome with a skirt, you will use the same basic wrapping techniques that you would with a boy gnome to make the legs — but you need to stop before you start the arms. Stop at the place where the pipe cleaner looks like an upside-down Y.

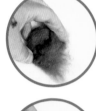

2   Using the color of wool you want for the skirt, roll the wool into a flattened circle — as if you are rolling a flat snail shell. Make sure to check the size — if it is too big, the skirt will be too large for the gnome. Remember that the radius of your circle is the length of the skirt. Start poking away at the circle, but you *must* remember to keep flipping the circle over to felt the other side, too. Otherwise it will felt into the felting pad. Once in a while, poke the edge all the way around the circle to tuck in the fibers and smooth out the edge.

3   Once the skirt is looking like a solid, flat circle, pick it up, fold it in half, and poke it about six times so that the needle penetrates both folded layers. You want to poke it where you imagine the waist of the skirt to be — this would be the halfway point on the folded edge. This little bit of felting helps the skirt take shape so it doesn't stick straight out.

4   Once you've made a couple of pokes at the invisible waistband area, pick up the skirt, shape it into a cone with your fingers, and pinch that area you imagine to be the waist of the skirt into the peak of the cone. Holding the open end of the cone (and keeping your fingers away), poke around the peak of the cone where the waist area is. Give it about twelve pokes. If you felt it up too much, it will be tricky to do the next steps.

5   Using a pair of scissors, snip a *tiny* slit at the peak of the little cone. The cone does not have to hold its tight cone shape when you let it go, but it will be more

cone-ish than it was before. Then, using the pointier side of the scissors, poke a hole all the way through the skirt in the place where you snipped the slit. This is the hole that your pipe cleaner will go through to attach the skirt to the gnome.

6   Put the pipe cleaner (the tail of the upside-down Y) through the hole you made in your skirt. Carefully push the skirt down until it rests over the legs where the tail of the Y ends and becomes the legs.

7   Using the same methods explained in the directions for making a boy gnome, make the arms for this gnome.

8   To put a shirt on or create the top of a dress, you will first attach the head the way you do with the boy gnome and put a shirt on the girl just as you would a boy gnome. To make the skirt into a dress, just use the same color wool for the shirt that you did for the skirt.

Making Striped Leggings or Pants

1 To put on striped leggings, begin by putting pants on your gnome just like you would normally. But when that is done, take a thin strip of the color of wool that you want the stripes to be, wrap it around the waist twice, and start wrapping it widely around the leg down to the ankle.

2 Once you reach the ankle, wrap it completely around once, then come back up the leg to the waist, wrap it once or twice around the waist, and felt it gently into the waist to hold it. Repeat for the other leg. You can then go down each leg and needle felt the stripes a bit to hold them in place. Now you have striped leggings!

Making Braids

1   To put braids on a gnome, you need three short (about 1 to 2 inches) strands of wool. Remember: The thicker the strands, the thicker the braid. Anchor the strands with a felting needle pushed deeply into the felting pad. Don't pull too hard since the felting needle can break or pull out. The braiding may take a couple of tries — wool can tear apart sometimes — but if you are gentle, you will get the hang of it!

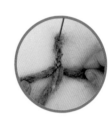

2   Once the braid is as long as you want it, take a thin strand of colorful wool and use it as a tie. Double-knot it to make sure it stays on, then gently needle felt the tie in place and needle felt the end of the braid to help it stay together. Repeat these instructions to create a second braid.

3 Carefully position the braid on the side of the head. The tuft at the beginning of the braid that the felting needle held in place while you were braiding is what you will be felting onto the side of the head. Look at your gnome, imagine where you think a braid would go, and then carefully felt the braid in place. Repeat this on the other side.

4 Attach the hat the same way you would on a boy gnome. Check the hairline and try to balance the hat so that it sits nicely on top of the head with the braids hanging down on either side.

Putting Polka Dots on a Hat

1   To put polka dots on a hat, simply take small tufts of wool in the color you want your dots and poke them into the hat. You will need to play with wool amounts to create the size of polka dots you want. Too little and they may poke too far into the hat and be invisible; too much wool and they may be far larger than you want. So play around with this and have fun!

Making a Baby Gnome or "Gnomeling"

1   Take a small, narrow piece of wool in the skin color of your choice. Using the technique shown in the boy gnome directions, roll this strip of wool into a small ball. Felt the tiny ball carefully, turning constantly to keep it round. Felting tiny things increases the risk that you might poke yourself, so go slowly and carefully. Leave the tail of the head (the part that looks like the tail of a comet) extra long. This will also be used to make the body.

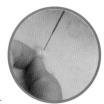

2   Use your thumb to hold the head and tail in place. Take the tail of the comet and start wrapping it around itself, starting at the base of the head where the neck would be. You are going to try to get the wool to wrap around itself and create a sort of pill shape to create the body of the baby. If the body gets too big, unwrap some of the wool and tear off the extra. Felt the body carefully, turning it

frequently so that it stays round and so that any rogue fibers get tucked into the body. Poke the needle around the base of the head where the neck would be to create a nice indentation for the neck.

3   Choose a color for your gnomeling's bunting and cover the body with this color wool, starting at the neck and working down. Felt the wool in place. Use additional tufts of wool to patch any places where the underlying skin tone shows through.

4   To cover the head, take a small tuft of the wool you chose for the bunting and drape it over the head. Place it so that the baby's face is shown. You may want to turn the head until you find the place you think the face should be and start from there. Felt this wool in place. Use the needle to poke around the face and neck to create a defining indentation for the hairline and neckline.

5 To add eyes, carefully poke two indentations where you wish the eyes to be. Take tiny tufts of black wool and poke them into these indentations.

6 Lastly, add hair by choosing a small tuft of the color wool you wish to use and carefully felting it at the peak of the forehead in the place where the bunting hood meets the face.

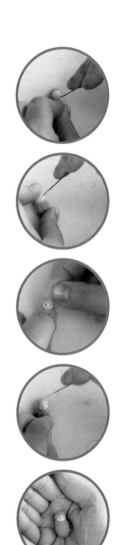

Acknowledgments

The appreciation and respect I have for my agent and my editor should never go without saying. I send out an abundance of gratitude to my agent, Laurie Abkemeier, who was supportive from the very beginning — without her insights, guidance, and faith in this book, I don't know what I would have done. And to my editor, Ann Treistman, who jumped with enthusiasm into this project and fueled it with her amazing energy, bringing this book to fruition. Thank goodness these two fabulous ladies were there to keep me smiling and laughing through this adventure!

I would like to send out enormous thank-yous: To my children and husband for their patience while I was distracted and absorbed in working on this book and for their tolerance of all the times I have said (and will likely say again) the words, "Oh — I have to make a gnome!" To my brother, who spent countless hours in front of a computer, going through the hundreds of gnome photos and cross-checking them for me. To my mother, who told me from an early age that I could make anything (and I really mean *anything* — including shoes!) — even when I had my doubts. To my father, who told me that it takes twenty-eight days to make a habit and twenty-eight days to break one — perhaps not an exact science, but it made me keep trying. To Diana, whose love of these gnomes not only fueled my faith in myself (and the gnomes) but also helped my family through some tough times. To Jackie, who helped fan (and feed) the flickering flame of inspiration when I was certain it was about to go out. To my soul sister, CJ, who once asked me the essential question: "What would you do if you knew you could not fail?"

Without the support, guidance, and love that I received along the way, so much in this life — including this book — would not have been possible. Thank you, thank you, thank you!

About the Author

Jessica Peill-Meininghaus grew up surrounded by art. Every lamp had been found at a flea market and re-covered with fabrics; every piece of Oriental rug was put to use in some form or another. Creativity was part of the very fabric of her childhood.

When she wet-felted her first piece, a ball, at the age of sixteen, she was hooked. After spending time creating wet-felted gnomes and tapestries, she came across needle felting and was suddenly able to lend more detail to her work than ever before.

Jessica has been selling her artwork for more than a decade. In addition to gnomes, she makes felted tapestries (also called "wool paintings"), felted books, felted coasters, felted tea and coffee press cozies, and custom felted banners.

Jessica and her husband live with their four children in Maine. When she isn't felting, Jessica raises her children, dreams of community-created art projects, and tends to the family's menagerie of animals. Visit her at www.themoongoat.com.